surf lessons

What readers are saying about *Surf Lessons*...

Surf Lessons changed my life in so many wonderful ways. It reminded me that real wealth flows from my own true nature. Nona's loving guidance and support transformed how I see myself, my life, and the world around me. I am happier and more fulfilled than I have been in years.

If the idea of engaging your heart and mind to create a richer life for yourself appeals to you, I highly recommend *Surf Lessons*.
— Cindy Connors, Life Coach

Surf Lessons is what I imagine the ocean to be. On the surface, it is a joyous experience of exploring and playing. But under the surface resides depth and new discovery that might go unnoticed if one remained above the waves, unwilling to dive deep.

Nona Jordan made it possible for me to play on the surface, splashing in the waves, and also to dive deep, discovering the powerful messages of deep and sacred play.
— Michelle Radomski, Graphic Designer

Nona Jordan's *Surf Lessons* is an invigorating exploration that had me engaged from the start. Nona's warm and knowing guidance through metaphor, play and expanding one's familiar strategies out into the unknown had me examining my practices (and stuck feelings) from a completely fresh perspective.

Surf Lessons reminded me of just how much I am capable of, and I've been enjoying these practices long after the end. I just can't say enough good things.
— Laurie Nadeau, Artist

Nona's wisdom guided me to exactly where the answers are – within myself. In doing the exercises that encouraged me to connect with nature, I reunited with my own guidance and started a transformation of confidence and trust in myself that continues to grow to this day. Nona's strength and wisdom pour out of *Surf Lessons* in a beautiful way, giving the opportunity for real change.

— Tracy McNeme Carrothers

surf lessons

exploring the power of nature to
awaken your abundance

Nona Jordan

Although the author and publisher have made every effort to ensure that the information in this book was correct at press time, the author and publisher do not assume and hereby disclaim any liability to any party for any loss, damage, or disruption caused by errors or omissions, whether such errors or omissions result from negligence, accident, or any other cause.

To Erick and Clara:

for showing me that every moment is an invitation to experience the pulse and the pleasure of life. Thank you for surfing with me in all the ways.

I love you both deeply, madly and truly.

People who have faith in life are like swimmers who entrust themselves to a rushing river. They neither abandon themselves to its current nor try to resist it. Rather, they adjust their every movement to the watercourse, use it with purpose and skill, and enjoy the adventure.

~David Steindl-Rast[i]

About the Author

*N*ona Jordan is a master certified coach and teacher to creative and spiritually-oriented women in business. Her work is dedicated to women who want to build a life and a business of personal authority, joy and meaning. Nona believes it is every person's birthright to trust their deep knowing, inner strength and actions as a path to creating the life, the business and the world they most want.

Nona brings intuitive coaching, practical guidance, as well as radiant healing practices of embodiment to her clients, connecting women to their unshakable truth – body, breath and soul. Her approach invites women to move through the world, and engage with their work, in a whole new way.

Her greater vision is to leave a legacy of women who have the courage to speak up and to do the work they feel called to do – to live a life that reflects the truth that all of us are whole and resource-rich and primed for success.

Nona lives a joyful (except when it's not), adventurous, nomadic life of exploration with her husband, daughter and Kelsie the dog. Find out more about individual coaching and programs at <u>nonajordan.com</u>.

Contents

Introduction

You hold in your hands a collection of essays and invitations from the teachings that living near the ocean gifted me, first inspiring me to create my world-renowned virtual program and now this book. As a master life coach and teacher, I offer you not only my metaphors and interpretations but also invitations to explore the power of *natural abundance* for yourself, whether you live near the sea or not.

I tend to think of natural abundance as the rich, ever-present resources we possess naturally, the inner wealth that allows us to experience the abundance of the world and to take action in ways that amplify abundance. It's a state I find myself in when I am deeply connected to my body and what I refer to as my soul – a state of magnetism, creativity and joy.

Residing in Hawai'i affirmed that my greatest desire is to know life deeply. For my life to be a prayer, for my hours to be spent awake to what's alive in me and what's alive in the world. This is abundance in the truest sense of the word.

I don't wish to simply observe. I want to participate, heart open wide. Forget stoicism or transcendence of the human experience. There is a whole range of experience that I hold and cherish as they pulse through my body - from grief and anguish to the fire in my belly to profound pleasure and joy.

Maybe, like me, this idea of really living - of experiencing the rich pleasures of life: of play, laughter, fierce love and an open, tender heart - have been a little uncomfortable or completely off-limits for you. I didn't understand just how much I held myself away from engaging with life fully until we moved to Hawai'i. Even when I said yes to surfing, to hiking, to the blissful enjoyment of living, there was a niggle of uncertainty. Was I was really allowed to experience all of this goodness?

I know among the people I know and work with, there are these hidden pockets of self-denial. Ways that we've let culture tell us what we can and cannot have, do or be. I believe that's why true pleasure can be so uncomfortable for so many people. The story may be different, but the result is the same - people who've shut down their own access to pleasure, bliss, love, play and joy – which is our birthright of abundance as humans.

We are built to enjoy life - with a capacity for great love and incredible sorrow. So when I say "enjoy life" I am not referring to "indulgence", or, numbing out with wine or food or endless TV shows and calling that "enjoyment" - I'm talking about living. Open-hearted, vulnerable and heartbreaking living that embraces the capacity for deep and abiding pleasure and the sensual, very alive nature of all our emotions and the experiences available to us. It's messy. And beautiful. And it's what you are made of and made for.

We are born whole and complete with a wealth of resources and skills that are instinctual. Play and pleasure and problem-solving are instinctual - they also connect you deeply to creativity, growth and clarity, three things that 100% of the women I work with want to have access to at all time because this is the fluid energy that creates everything we want. This is the very wellspring of abundance.

I believe that you have the capacity to open your heart wide and say yes to life and to the world. I believe that you can let yourself have the experiences you wish to have, embrace it all, lean into life and love and pleasure.

Throughout this book, I invite you to consider whether you are allowing yourself the pleasure of living your life. I invite you to notice what you aren't doing that you long to do. You get to choose whether you fuel your life with the power of abundance or scarcity – I hope this book will inspire you to choose abundance.

My deepest wish is for you to feel enlivened and empowered through the words and invitations on these pages. For you to be inspired to explore your inner and outer landscapes with curiosity and joy. For you to embody the rich life that is available to you right now. For you to see, taste, touch and live a different story; a story that speaks the truth of personifying your state of natural abundance.

May my experience and these essays invite you to ride the waves of your own beautiful life with more play and ease.

How to Live the Practices in This Book

*H*ow many times have you picked up a book on personal development and nodded and agreed with what you read without actually DOING the prescribed exercises? For me, it's too many times to count. However, for anything to change you, you must act. So please don't just read it, do it. Most everything in life is transformative if you actually make a commitment – I so hope you will do just that with the invitations in *Surf Lessons.*

As my first invitation, I invite you to create daily sacred time for exploring these practices. Set aside time to savor the reading of one essay at a time as a gift you give to yourself, and it *will* pay dividends. Also:

- **Be present and open.** Look for synchrony, look for the support of the Universe through an abundance of signs before, during and after your Surf Lessons.

- **Be willing to risk.** Play at your edges. Step toward the thing(s) that scare you but excite you.

- **Notice what you notice** about your experience of yourself and of your life.

- **Take notes.** It's going to be juicy.

You are going to have fun if nothing else, but I believe you're going to experience SO much more than that.

xoxo . nona

nonajordan.com surf lessons

Prelude:
Let Yourself Play

*T*his is a radical idea: We can realize our natural abundance by making a fierce commitment to our own pleasure, to making space for play and our desires each day. I call these activities *Core Practices.*

What, exactly, are Core Practices? Core Practices are activities that feel absolutely delicious when you take time for them, and you take the time for one or more of them nearly every day.

As a person who has picked up *Surf Lessons*, you may, like me, be a woman who is acclimated to staying busy, putting everyone and everything else first. You may be very familiar with pain and suffering as the primary catalysts for growth. While you are surfing with me, I invite you to give pleasure, play and desire serious consideration as vehicles that can support transformation as well.

In the spirit of turning toward play, I'm going to invite you to create your own list of Core Practices that are unique to you. You likely already know some activities in your life that would fit the description of a Core Practice, right? My Core Practice Playlist includes walking or hiking in nature, surfing or boogie boarding, swimming in the ocean, river rafting, meditating outdoors, yoga, dancing, drawing

Zentangles, painting, journaling, drumming and singing. I find that the more visceral and full-body my practices are, the more they connect me, ground me and fill me up.

Core Practices are key to living from your natural abundance. Engaging in Core Practices throughout your Surf Lessons (and beyond) will support you in recognizing your capacity to have the life you desire in this very moment. There is something magical about making pleasure and play a top priority, because these are often things we put off, waiting for some magical condition to be met first. When you are nourishing yourself with pleasure through the Core Practices on your playlist, you are re-membering and connecting to creative energy, possibility, strength and your incredible human capacity to engage with life. You are reminding yourself daily that you get to choose to live from joy and your natural abundance.

Here's what I mean by that—

When you postpone play, you deny yourself a fundamental building block of living from your natural abundance. Make no mistake, play and pleasure are necessary forces of creation and evolution – consider how children come into this world. Sex is for pleasure 99% of the time; it is certainly not just for procreation or we wouldn't crave it. Play and pleasure are the heartbeat of creation and our innate capacity to create is at the core of living from natural abundance.

On the other end of the spectrum, when you make choices that drop you to the bottom of the list – because you are telling yourself you are too busy – you are embodying lack through your actions. So while you might be mentally inviting abundance, you are repelling it with actions that are based on a fundamental sense of scarcity. Will you ever feel a sense of abundance when you repeatedly do this? In my experience, no.

However, when you consciously choose yourself, what you love and what brings you pleasure, when you choose to go outdoors and connect with nature (which we are *so* meant to do), when you feel the full range of your feelings, when you move and create just because those actions feed you and feel good, and when you also choose to put yourself and your desires first? That is the very embodiment of abundance. With that, you will always have enough time, energy, attention and presence for what fills you up because you've said so by choosing yourself first.

Please remember as you embark on this journey that there is no perfect endgame to reach; it's a journey to find your own rhythm. It's messy, and it shifts constantly, like the tides. To find your rhythm requires you to be present to what is alive in this moment (instead of last month). I am very aware of how it feels when I am connected to my natural state of abundance through choosing pleasure, play and my Core Practices each day – and how it feels when I'm not.

I will mention that I spent a lot of years engaged in yoga, meditation and other indoor pursuits. When I connected with nature and got over my fear of going outside and being uncomfortable, I finally felt fully alive and connected to my innate natural abundance. Why would being inside versus outside make such a big difference? Because you and I, we *are* nature. Because we are nature, we need a direct connection with non-human nature to feel the incredible support of nature and the true depth of our intrinsic natural abundance.

As you engage with your Core Practices, may you find yourself inspired. Take your practices outdoors. Attune to nature within and all around and most important, choose yourself *first* to experience the unique currents of your natural abundance.

Whether or not you have selected your Core Practices (yet), in the first lesson you will explore which practices connect you to your source of natural abundance by *doing* practices of your choosing. This may feel awkward, but it will become less awkward in the doing.

I understand this is a radical choice, and I invite you to jump in. Make a commitment to connect to YOUR source of natural abundance through play, through delight. A daily practice that brings you pleasure has the effect of waking you up, inspiring action and amplifying your energy. Being awake, inspired and energized are THE keys to connecting to your best self, and not only experiencing, but living from, your natural abundance.

First Lesson:
Stop Waiting

*P*icture this:

I sit in front of my computer, feeling like I can't move. Going numb. Wanting to access more fluid energy, new ideas and more courage to be who I am meant to be, but I convince myself I cannot play until everything else is done. I have the familiar knot in the pit of my stomach.

"Everything" will never be done. The conditions can never be met. I will never feel like I can have what I really want if I do the same things over and over.

Does that sound familiar?

When we endeavor to find and stay connected to a state of natural abundance, we are waging a fierce revolution against societal norms. Everything about our culture wants us to stay slightly (or very) numb. To keep working endlessly, to keep consuming, and to keep striving for something that is slightly beyond our reach. This endless cycle keeps us tightly engaged in obligation and a sense that there will never be enough, be it time, energy, or money. The message is loud and clear: we surely do *not* have time for anything but the busy-ness that keeps us in this deadly cycle.

However, in my experience, the more you run on the gerbil wheel of obligation, the more you'll want to indulge yourself with "treats" for working so damned hard. You will indulge yourself for being a "good girl" but your indulgence is just another sign that you feel a sense of lack. These "treats" are a poor substitute for what you really seek – like eating aspartame instead of sugar. And guess what?

Obligation, busy-ness and "have to's" kill your creative energy and you probably aren't going to do your most brilliant work in that environment. That will likely lead you to feel like you aren't enough because, on some level, you aren't. Unless you are consciously, actively connecting to YOUR source of natural abundance every day, you aren't truly your most brilliant, clear and creative self. That feeling of not-enough is your higher-self begging you to connect back to your natural abundance.

On the day I really "got it", and I committed to connecting with my natural abundance daily I didn't know what happen; I just took the leap. I committed. I reached out to a friend, asked her if she wanted to learn to surf, and then I wrote this poem:

> *Today, I am going to stop waiting for my husband to retire, for my thighs to be thinner, for my bank account to be thicker, and for sure I'm going to stop waiting for my complement of offers to be more robust.*

Today (and please, dear Goddess, every day from here on out)

I'm going to devour my life. Eat it whole.

Let the juice dribble down my chin.

Allow myself the luxury of the sticky mess.

Laugh uproariously.

Love hard.

Play even harder.

Share all of myself.

Follow the inspiration in my work.

Delight in the mundane.

Change my mind when I please.

Nap in the hammock every day.

Dance under the light of the moon.

Interpret the symbols that are all around me.

Walk with my luminous angels and my beautiful demons.

Embrace that every fucking moment is sacred, sacred, sacred.

The list? It goes on.

If you were to stop waiting, what would you do?

To be the person you are meant to be in this day and age of possibility and promise -- your creative energy, your light and your clarity are needed most.

We find those precious resources NOT in front of a computer, or by doing busy work, but by finding our source, our connection, in daily play and daily practices that feed our energy.

A Note on Play and Rest:

We live in a chronically exhausted society. So what do you do if your definition of play is really active but you are really tired? Or physically or mentally ill?

Play and rest are not at all mutually exclusive, but when exhaustion or physical issues are a factor, you will need to open your mind to more possibilities around what play can mean for you.

For example, when my energy is low, I often go outdoors to walk with my camera, or I will journal or create art. In times of low energy, those activities are my play. I have also gone through particularly challenging times when daily naps were my priority. Make no mistake, napping is deeply pleasurable and is definitely on my list of Core Practices.

I wonder what super-restful activities would feel playful and pleasurable for you?

As you select and arrange your Core Practices, consider putting restful, nourishing Core Practices first. These calming, nurturing Playlist activities will serve you well throughout *Surf Lessons* and beyond.

You Are Invited:
Stop Waiting

The heart and soul of Surf Lessons are taking a risk and choosing yourself, by putting play and Core Practices first to connect you to your unique currents of natural abundance.

Let's define your unique practice Playlist. These activities connect you (or get you closer) to a state of natural abundance by filling you up, clearing your head and bringing you joy.

As you continue reading this book, you are encouraged to gift yourself at least one practice every day. Even if it's for only 10 or 15 minutes, by doing this you are affirming an abundance of time and energy to put play first.

Suggestions for Your Practice Playlist

- Activities on the Practice Playlist should be unrelated to work or craft. No matter how much you love what you do or how creative and playful it feels, it's essential the practices allow you to walk away and experience the world through a different lens
- Consider making at least one (preferably more) of your Practices something you do outdoors.

Having trouble?

Not quite sure what you would enjoy having on your Practice Playlist? Think of it as crafting the most awesome, rocking list of songs . . . oooh, that's play too.

So let's talk about play for a moment—

Sometimes we think of play as being childlike or childish behavior – mainly, I believe, because we tend to leave the whole concept of play behind as we grow older. If you look up the word *play* in the dictionary – wow – you'll find there is a lot to take in, from musical instruments to embodying a role for theater. But the zoological definition of play is the simplest—

> *Actions that have all the elements of purposeful behavior but are performed for no apparent reason.*

If you are struggling to come up with activities you enjoy, that are playful for YOU, I invite you to define play for yourself. Start with the feeling-state of play. What does play feel like for you?

For me, play feels open, present, curious and connected. Also, it's *much* easier for me to access playful feeling states when I go outdoors or I connect with the nature within myself – my emotions and my intuition and my body. That is one of the reasons I highly encourage you to take your practice outdoors.

So what activities that may be done for no apparent reason bring you to your ideal feeling-state? As you go through this book and play around with your practices, I recommend you take note of which activities plug you into a natural feeling of abundance.

Stumped on what natural abundance might feel like? I can't tell you what it will feel like for you in definitive terms, however, in my experience, you'll know a unique expression of natural abundance and recognize the vast resources that are within, as well as in the world around you. It's your personal experience of the power to choose, your bright mind, your strong body, your instincts, your desires, your senses and your connection to the world. You'll come to know this state intimately because you were born with it.

If you are struggling to define your Practice Playlist, here are ideas to consider:

- What did you love to do as a child?
- What activities bring you a deep sense of pleasure?
- What have you wanted to try but haven't made time for yet?

Start there. Be gentle with yourself, and pick one or three of the things you come up with as a Practices-To-Try-Playlist.

Stay open, stay curious and (wait for it) stay playful as you explore your daily practices and notice how they make you feel.

Interlude

Finding your own way IS the only right way.

One woman said of her own Playlist—

"I am realizing that for me the best way to play is to BE. For me putting play on the list ends up to be 'work' in about 5 seconds. So I put away the 'playlist', and I decided to embrace playing minute by minute. I know that to play I must show up for myself ... for my body ... for my life. I must be present.

So I am choosing to BE a playful person. I am being open and present and curious and loving for as much of my day as possible.

I am being more playful with my work, my husband, my morning walks, even my breath. Sometimes I just stop for 5 seconds and 'play' with how I am breathing. (Can I breathe into my toes? Oh, yes. Look, I can. Can I breathe into my fingernails, my hair, my ears?) It is just a fun way of Being. I am so excited about this process.

I am BEING a person who plays. This is not something I would have said two weeks ago." ~Michelle Radomski, Graphic Designer

Lesson Two:
Terror and Excitement
Hold Hands on the Beach

*P*icture this:

I'm hanging back in the ironwood grove that stands at the back of the beach. I'm watching the instructors get ready for the day. They haven't seen me, I could still leave and go home. Pretend this never happened.

After I hit puberty, I became a girl who did not try new things. In many ways, I went inside, and I closed the door. I embraced the societal message that, as a woman, I wasn't safe in the world. For a long time, I didn't do things that I felt put my safety at risk, made me look stupid or would cause me to fail in front of others. I was a dedicated perfectionist, married to my desire to look good and stay safe at all costs. Being an entrepreneur and a coach, and moving all over the world, has cured me of much of those tendencies – but not entirely.

> *I can barely breathe, I'm so nervous. I feel excitement and I feel terror all in one pulsing, pounding wave of emotion. I remind myself to stay relaxed, to stay open, that I'm DEFINITELY going to fall in and look ridiculous AND that it doesn't*

matter because I'm doing something new.

But I still have the urge to walk away.

Deciding to take a surf lesson?

Definitely leaning into my edge.

Catastrophic thoughts run through my mind: Will I be safe? Is this too much for me? Can I do it? What if I fail? What if I love it? Am I going to look stupid?

With a deep inhale, I take my fear by the hand and step onto the beach. The terror is there and so is the excitement. There is room for both as I step forward and take the risk to learn to surf. I have the capacity to

hold both of those competing emotions
and still take action.

That day, I fell off the board more times than I stood up. I badly scraped my thigh on coral during a tumble. I was sore and exhausted by the end of my 2-hour lesson. But I stood up. I caught a wave. When I stepped out of the water, I felt like a new woman. I had a new faith in myself and my capacity to risk, to do hard things, to do scary things.

I felt alive in a way I haven't felt since I was a child – I reforged a connection to my natural abundance that had been lost long ago.

Surfing is one of the best things I ever did for myself, my daughter, my marriage and my business.

Why? Because most everything beautiful is risky, from honest conversations with our loved ones to learning to rock climb, and everything we really want is out beyond our field of fears and doubts. The decision to take a courageous step forward is critical. It is exhilarating to say Yes to those desires that lie at the edges of your comfort zone.

When you try new things, play at the edges, you hone the ability to hold fear lightly. Instead of letting fear stop you, you get comfortable with risk and failure (which are always a part of doing new things) and, most important, you foster bravery and the ability to take risks in "real" life.

Not only that, it's fun. Bonus.

You Are Invited:
What Would Take Your Breath Away?

Today I invite you to name twenty activities you would do for play, for fun – things that feel risky. What activities elicit a quickened heartbeat and a rush of excitement?

Where would you go? What would you try? What would you choose?

Make sure to look around your immediate environment, look for activities that are available to you this very second (or at least in the immediate future) instead of pursuits that have hurdles or put up more roadblocks.

Notice the judgments or the excitement, or both, that arrive and the thoughts that wash up with them. Observe carefully and with curiosity, so you come to recognize and understand your inner predators.

surf lessons

Lesson Three:
Drop the Conditions

*T*he ocean is not about certainty. It calls up something entirely different in us – shows us the folly of insisting on solid ground.

Picture this:

> *I am kicking out toward my favorite snorkel spot, pushing against the current that pulls me back and forth as I make my way through this underwater playground – the*

gorgeous reef off the west side of Oahu.

I spot a sea turtle and decide to shift my course, letting myself drift with the current, taking the turtle's lead.

As I drift in the ocean, letting the ebb and flow of the current carry me, I am struck by my vacillation between lack and abundance, even here in this ocean playground. Feeling tight and contracted around my need to "get somewhere"(the spot I originally had in mind) before I can drop in and really enjoy myself (hanging out with the turtle). The lack happens in my mind; the abundance is always here.

I am struck by how often I needlessly place conditions between myself and what I want: WHEN I have more clients, unpack all the boxes, clean the toilets, have a million dollars in the bank or { insert your own condition here } ... THEN I will surf, snorkel, meditate, feed myself, travel, speak my truth, cry or { insert your own version of love and play here }. "THEN" never comes but "not enough" doesn't leave – until you connect with your innate, lush source of abundance.

Here with this turtle, I choose to strip away the complex series of rewards and conditions I impose on myself. Here I decide to follow the love, the joy, the breadcrumbs, the hot tracks on the path to connecting with my natural abundance. This is the energy and the inspiration I want to fuel my day-to-day life on land.

I choose to challenge the conditions: the Shoulds, Have Tos and Must Dos that I find in my path.

The ocean continually reminds me that conditions are a feeble attempt to create a false sense of certainty which doesn't exist in the ocean or on dry land. No solid ground, just me and the current.

As I've committed to dropping conditions, I have noticed fear and hesitancy. A certain superstitious knowing that I would fail and my world would fall apart if I actually dropped the conditions I carefully place on myself, my business, my happiness and my life. Some days, it feels profoundly risky to drop the conditions and go with the current of play and desire – the pathways to the source of natural abundance.

Despite my fear, the evidence continues to build in favor of dropping conditions. My business and my bank accounts continue to grow – and, in fact, they are growing more quickly than ever since I've committed to choosing myself and dropping conditions. I am a better wife and parent – more willing to say No (and Yes, for that matter) and have hard conversations with both my husband and my daughter. When I choose to do something, I do it. And most important, I'm happier. Simply because I decided to challenge the idea that certain conditions must be met to access the joy and abundance that is already mine for the taking.

Here's the thing: The practices, risks and activities that get put on hold? The moments of connection that take a backseat to conditions? They hold the key to finding and living from natural abundance.

Try it and see.

Interlude

Money becomes such a condition. All we can see is we need more money, there isn't enough – that is the direction we look in and our vision becomes myopic.

However, what if you were to look around with an eye to adventure and play and explore what is available with what you have now? Hiking, skinny dipping in a lake or river you've hiked to, or sleeping out under the stars.

You may have a desire to take a class or do something that requires money AND I wonder . . . if you were to open up your lens and cast your net wider, see what's available to you that would feel like play and abundance without money, I wonder if you might be surprised at the abundance you find.

P.S. You could also bring some playful energy to the money situation. IF you needed $10,000 in three days, what would you do? What would you sell? What could you offer?

When the conditions are dropped, you're open to possibilities, expanding the limitless capacities.

You Are Invited:
Drop the Conditions

Whatever conditions you have falsely set for yourself, I invite you to drop them.

At this point, you may already hear the whispers of conditions or fears as they pop in to say that you can't get to your Core Practices or that something else should be completed first- then maybe you find you don't get to the practice at all.

No need to get angry at yourself, this is rich and valuable information for you – it's also completely human, so you can give yourself a break. If you approach your resistance with compassion and curiosity, it will lead you straight to the hidden-in-plain-sight conditions you've carried around and lived with for years.

Exercise: Rewriting Your Shoulds

First, pull out a sheet of paper and down the left side make a list of all the things you "should" do, "have to" do, "must" do or "can't" do. Let loose. If you are having trouble getting to your daily Core Practice, make sure to write down all the things that "have to" come before your daily Play time.

Example:

I *should* finish the laundry

I *have* to pack their lunches

I *must* put on makeup

I *can't* go to dance class

Next, on the right side of your sheet of paper, rewrite each "should", "have to", "must" or "can't" do statement and replace the conditional words *should, have to, must* and *can't* with the words *WANT TO*.

Example:

I *should* finish the laundry	I **want to** finish the laundry
I *have to* pack their lunches	I **want to** pack their lunches
I *must* put on makeup	I **want to** put on makeup
I *can't* go to dance class	I **want to** go to dance class

It may be that you don't want to finish the laundry, but you *do* want folded clothes to wear – it's entirely possible that you want the outcome even if you don't want to do the task. Use this exercise to challenge yourself, to notice how much you put your desires at the bottom of the list or put things on your to-do list that you don't need to do or don't really want to do. Cross anything off the list that isn't a genuine want or that doesn't have a genuinely desired outcome.

Now, get out there and give yourself permission to play first, Surfer Girl.

Lesson Four:
Paddle Out Into the Waves

*P*icture this:

Today is a surf day. There is a really big swell hitting the island right now. I notice as I walk onto the beach with my board that the waves are bigger than normal today.

The most important thing a surf instructor will tell you before you hit the water is to steer the nose of your board straight into the waves. Don't hesitate. Meet that wave head on; otherwise, the wave will get the upper hand and likely dump you off your board.

As I pushed my board into the water this morning, I paddled straight out, right into the waves. The faces of many of the waves were big – so big that a lot of them crashed over me and my board, leaving me wet, breathless, and ultimately, laughing. Mostly I was able to stay on my board while paddling out, but the few waves where I hesitated? I found myself rolled off my board.

Paddling out is the critical first action that takes you through your fear and out to the unknown, toward the edge. This is where the growth happens. This is where our limits expand. This is where we foster trust in ourselves and connect to the natural abundance of resources within and all around us.

Now it's your turn to paddle out into the waves – to take the risk.

Interlude

I took my daughter to the Big Island. The risk piece for me was swimming at night with the giant manta rays. I once scuba-dove at night, and it completely creeped me out and since then, I've stayed out of and away from the ocean at night.

So I went ahead, and I took my daughter.

We took a boat out to the ray feeding spot and jumped into the water. We shone lights into the depths so the little luminescent creatures the manta rays eat would congregate around us.

Then the rays came. Huge rays. Big eight- to twelve-foot wing spans doing this exquisite ballet, swimming in giant loops with their mouths open wide. One looped so close to me I could have pursed *my lips as if to kiss my beloved and my lips would have brushed its belly.*

It was mesmerizing. Watching them, the darkness fell away. I was surprised at how unafraid I was in the moment — all the 'what ifs' and fear fell away. And it was a magnificent experience to share with my daughter, who was also a little nervous.

Every single time I do something just because I want to, just because it sounds amazing, just because it tugs at my heart — every time I do something for no reason other than to know the world around me in a new way, I am blessed with a deeper understanding of the beauty of the world, my choice in how I engage with it, my innate abundance of resources and, of course, myself as part of nature.

So who cares about experiencing beauty, right? Well, here's how this is weaving its way into the way I live my life —

I've often felt like I don't fit – that, somehow, I just never belong. I'm too practical to be in the witches and hippies campouts, and I'm too wild and natural to be put in the penthouse or the boardroom.

But, somehow, experiencing the landscape of an active volcano and the amazing creatures off the coast of the Big Island, I found that my liminal, in-between place is a place in and of itself. To be able to travel between both spaces – what a gift. I am infinitely practical and earthy and grounded AND I have a strong intuition and trust in what cannot be seen. It's who I am, and trying to be one or the other is what makes me feel like I don't belong.

Newfound acceptance of where I belong = greater acceptance of my deepest and truest superpower – the ability to walk between both worlds and the value of integrating the two. Volcanos don't apologize for their nature. As a being of nature myself, why would I?

As a result, I can already sense the stirrings of things changing in my business – I often find myself toning it down and that feels unacceptable now.

For example, I was asked to teach for a fellow coach's program, and she asked me to submit a short one-sentence mantra, of sorts, that sums me up. My first one was very acceptable, very soft and gentle. The host emailed me to ask if that was really what I wanted to say. My reply: NO.

After it had been rewritten, it felt so much more authentic to who I am and how I show up for people.

All because I'm committed to play and risk and connecting to the wisdom of nature. No seeming connection, yet nature is my tarot. My body is my divination tool. Play instructs my business plan.

This is an unexpected pathway to understanding the depths of my natural abundance.

What gifts are nature and play offering you?

You Are Invited:
Paddle Out

We find aliveness and power not from what contains, locates and protects us, but from what dissolves, reveals and expands us.

~Eve Ensler[ii]

For this lesson, as you continue the practice of play each day, step out of your comfort zone to move through and beyond the field of conditions or fears that have held you back.

During our second lesson, you explored trying new things and/or being mindful to give yourself permission to do activities you love (but don't do nearly as often as you would like). Now, are you ready to set a date with a take-your-breath-away experience of your choosing?

This isn't about doing something dangerous or life-threatening. In fact, I would NOT encourage that at all. This is about doing something you've wanted to do, something on your list from Lesson Two that will take your breath away when you do it. An exciting activity that you've put conditions around or you've been putting off.

In my experience, when you step to the edges of your fear and take on risk and adventure, the following happens:

1) You experience more creative juice, more aliveness, more clarity,

2) You feel more courageous and brave in other aspects of your life, and

3) You experience a felt sense of your capacity and resilience that is not dependent on conditions.

So let's do this thing. Today is your day to make a plan. Pull out pen and paper and write down what you've chosen to do – what you're no longer going to put off or put conditions on. Next, get specific. Set your date with the waves. When will you paddle out? Who will you do it with? What do you need to prepare? As you write out your plan of action, notice your feelings of excitement and fear and also express those in words.

surf lessons

Lesson Five:
Choose

*I*t's easy to talk ourselves out of it.

Right after I got my very own surfboard, I decided I was going to go out by myself for "Dawn Patrol" – the early morning, sunrise surf.

I was SO excited. I prepared meticulously. The car was packed with my favorite bathing suit at the ready. I woke up before the sun, ate breakfast and took a cup of coffee to go. I was so sure of myself as I drove to the beach.

When I arrived, the sun was rising over Diamond Head in the distance, the clouds pink and gold over the Ko'olau mountains. There were only men on the beach at that early hour, a handful of them already out on the waves. Everyone knew everyone, greeting each other with easy smiles and chatting comfortably.

I drank my coffee; the knot in my stomach grew tighter. I was afraid to go out by myself. I felt alone and very…new.

I couldn't do it.

I turned around, got in my car and drove home.

I cried the whole way.

When I got home, my husband was surprised to see me, and he sympathized as I let out the torrent of fear. He told me I could sell the board, give up, the culture of surfing wasn't for me – right? Right??

There were multiple reasons to give up, to walk away, to not do the scary thing. But when I thought about NOT surfing I felt sad and fractured, weak, my chest caved in. It felt horrible. I couldn't choose to give up.

I decided to go back out, but in a way that felt MUCH safer for me. In fact, I took my husband – who fell in love with surfing too.

There are always reasons not to do what we want to do – it's SO easy to talk ourselves out of it. We can throw up barriers and excuses or we can find a way through the detours (both internal and external) to move closer to our dreams.

After surfing many times with my husband, my daughter and a friend, I found myself putting my surfboard in the car once again for Dawn Patrol. That time, I didn't talk myself out of it. That time, I didn't leave.

It took me a little longer than I originally anticipated to get there – but who cares? I chose myself. I chose to continue. I chose to take a risk BUT with some extra support.

Blessing

by Jan Richardson[iii]

What we choose changes us.
Who we love transforms us.

How we create remakes us.
Where we live reshapes us.

So in all our choosing
...make us wise;

in all our loving,
...make us bold;

in all our creating,
...give us courage;

in all our living
may we become whole.

Interlude

Yesterday I was talking with a fellow surfer about contrast — how hard it can feel to play and how easy it is to choose less, to tell ourselves a story about how play is not important.

I have MANY days where I don't play, but I don't beat myself up — after all, I'm a recovering workaholic. What I've learned through that contrast is when I don't choose me, when I get knotted up in the "work harder, do more, obligations, shoulds, etc.," I feel that tense emptiness of not enough. I feel disconnected from my natural abundance.

I don't beat myself up, I notice and get curious.

Here is the thing: We live in a world where we are all conditioned to be good boys and girls, to buck up and sit down and do our work because that is the path to success. We are told that is the way we will gain enough money, accolades, security – name your price.

I love my work. It brings me great joy. Mostly, work, for me feels like play. BUT at the same time, if I don't choose the lush abundance of pleasure first – if I decide not to play, if I let myself slip to the bottom of the list, if I let conditions prevent me from connecting with the nature within and all around me – I go awry

My internal alignment falters, and while my clarity is still good, it's not the eagle vision I have with play, and I am not as present to my life. In accessing nature, in choosing play, in valuing the instinctual pleasures of being alive, I become fortified with wisdom and insight into how to take actions that make my dreams manifest. I'm then open to outcomes and I trust the process.

To me, this is playful AND it's a serious choice. It's a choice NOT to toe the line we've all been taught to toe. Choosing to embody abundance, to tap into your true nature and the nature all around you is a revolution.

So as you choose to embody abundance, notice and stay curious. Be kind and open to yourself. If you aren't feeling it, relax the muscles of your face, take a deep breath and try something else – PLAY with it.

Sometimes it is hard to make the choice – every ounce of your being may be in resistance or throwing up walls. So put on some music and dance with that resistance – feel it, get to know it, play with it and move right through it. Drop the judgment. Honor the contrast. Keep it easy and let it move you.

You Are Invited:
Choose

What are you choosing?

Our choices define us, make us into the person we are and will become.

> What will you choose today?

> Will you choose to play?

> To adventure?

> To take the scary step?

> To take your own breath away?

In what ways can you support yourself in stepping out of your comfort zone?

Lesson Six:
Play at Your Edges

*T*he more you play at your edges, the more confident you will be and the wider and deeper your comfort zone becomes.

Reefs are dark and craggy places with jagged edges and hidden dangers that hold unspeakable beauty. The best surfing and the best snorkeling (at least off of the island of Oahu) seem to be found in places where it's somewhat, if not downright, risky to play.

Picture this:

The sun is shining bright this morning, and I've taken my daughter, Clara, out of school for a surf lesson. A hurricane is scheduled to impact our island and the shores over the next few days, promising Big Surf. My stomach flip-flops as alerts on my phone announce the hurricane watch, and I wonder if it's wise to take my daughter into the water today. Perhaps it would be wiser to stay home. Perhaps not.

When we get to the beach, the waves are so puny the lessons are cancelled, but I can feel that the waves racing toward the shore are disorganized in a way they usually aren't. I feel brave just floating in the water today, knowing a big storm is churning in waters not far away.

The more I take risks in the ways I play and engage with the world, the more confident I become in all aspects of my life, and the less fear and conditions prevent me from diving toward my edges. When I challenge myself, I come to know myself more deeply as the heroine of the story I author with each passing moment. Knowing this connects me to deeper facets of my natural abundance, particularly my innate strength in the face of my precious and fragile humanity.

My experience tells me that playing at the edge nurtures confidence as we brush up against the uncertainty of life and the darker places we tend to avoid. Through risk, we say "yes" to the deep mysteries of life and the creative darkness that light seemingly doesn't penetrate. We come back from these edges renewed and connected to our wisest, most capable nature. This edge-diving cultivates a bone-deep knowledge of our resilience and an unshakable belief in our vast capacity for embracing the full spectrum of living.

You Are Invited:
Play at Your Edges

With the previous two lessons you chose a risk and made a play-full action plan to accomplish it, and you also explored and experienced your feelings around the contrast of choosing.

Now, the risk you chose for yourself is the edge you will play at with this lesson.

Remember: When you take risks through play you may,

1) Experience more creativity, presence, and confidence,

2) Feel more audacious and brave in other aspects of your life, and

3) Experience a felt sense of competence and strength that is not dependent on conditions.

My hope is you will dive toward your chosen risk, into your desire, and play at your edge victoriously – note I did not say *gracefully* or *fearlessly*.

I also hope you will recognize how this builds stronger connections to your natural abundance, and that you feel your innate strength and courage ripple out into other areas of your life as a result of taking this risk.

> *P.S. After you take your risk, here are some questions to help you integrate and process your experience . . . and, of course, keep on keepin' on with*

your daily Core Practices, which are the heart and soul of living from your natural abundance.

After the Risk

You took the risk, you challenged your fears, conditions and judgments and you played at your edge. Did you take your own breath away? I hope so because I'm totally impressed.

Take some time to answer these questions. Articulating your experience will help you celebrate and embrace the power of your experience.

- What "edge" did you choose for yourself?
- What judgment or inner criticism did you notice? What fears, judgments, and conditions did you challenge, release and/or walk with through your experience?

- Tell your story. Write about your Take Your Breath Away experience.
- What did you notice around you?
- What did you notice in yourself?
- Do you see your experience reflected in other parts of your life/business?
- What are your big takeaways from this experience?
- What are you celebrating about your experience?
- Are there additional questions this experience is inspiring you to ask?

nonajordan.com surf lessons

Lesson Seven:
Finding the Treasure

There is nothing but divine movement in this world.

~Hafiz[iv]

*F*inding the treasure is simply a matter of curiosity, openness and presence.

When I first began surfing, I would have told you there were no beaches worth going to nearby. However, there is a beach called White Plains the locals go to exactly eight minutes from my home. It's deep in an old military base, so getting there isn't pretty – rusty fences and dilapidated buildings overgrown with vines, and the nearby water treatment facility often smells pretty bad.

It's a place not even worth mentioning, let alone a place to look for treasures, right?

Now I know that nearby beach holds *infinite* treasures. I walk it, surf it or swim in its waves multiple times each week. I've even come to treasure the not-so-beautiful drive to the beach. I love seeing the ways Nature is winning as she slowly decomposes and swallows the old military buildings. I love the way the sky opens up and the wildness of the island shows through when I get away from the housing development and out into that seeming no man's land. I love that the birds have open spaces to nest and feed. I love how the turn to the beach is unmarked, off a bumpy road and you have to know where it is to find it.

Then there is the beach itself, with a view to Diamond Head that is to die for and consistent sets of waves, five or six waves deep. Smiling faces. Happy children. Monk seals. Incredible tide pools teeming with life. Lava ledges pounded by surf and punctuated with permanent altars to those who have died in the waves. All under light breezes and ever-shifting clouds.

Endless treasure.

If you asked me a year ago, I would've told you it wasn't worth your time, or mine, to go there. But then I got curious and opened up to receive the treasure right under my nose. Now it's one of my most favorite places to access my natural abundance. My fervent wish is to be given eyes to see what is all around me so I may, through play and wonder and delight, connect to the treasures that nature is always willing to generously provide.

Treasure is just waiting for you to recognize it in the form of beauty, of peace, of joy and delight, of insight, of wisdom. Whatever treasure you seek, it IS available and it is a vital connection to the source of your abundance.

These practices of deep play, risk, dancing at our edges, newness and openings… all of them: these are how we attune our inner knowing to those intuitive whispers that guide us and lead us forward in the sweet spot of connection to natural abundance.

You Are Invited:
A Treasure Hunt

This time you are invited to complete a Medicine Walk, where you will seek the treasures of clarity and insight for questions you ask. Know that finding your treasure is simply a matter of tuning in to the wisdom that is always just an intention or a question away when you connect to the nature within and all around you.

Today, I would invite you to start planning your very own Medicine Walk – the ultimate playful exploration of how Divine Source and the treasures you seek are always present when you are open to receiving what is waiting for you.

Medicine Walk: Receiving Answers to Your Questions

What questions do you seek answers to? I have found that nature – both within and all around – provides answers that are actionable and always lead me in the right direction to take the next step that is needed. This is a vital aspect of cultivating natural abundance: listening and trusting nature within and all around.

There are two ways you can play with receiving information and interpreting what you notice in non-human nature. Please, please, PLEASE use these as loose guidelines; if you have an inspiration or feel called to explore the wise counsel of nature in other ways, please do.

Medicine Walk Guidelines

Choose your outdoor destination: Whether you decide to meditate, hike, kayak, surf or do yoga, choose your outdoor destination before you go. Personally, I like to go somewhere a little wilder than my neighborhood, but there is no wrong answer here – I find plenty of guidance in the garden around my home.

Think about your energy levels and what would feel most delicious: to be in motion or not in motion. Choose accordingly. Make it awesome for yourself. When I was doing daily sits outdoors in Colorado, I would wrap myself up in a sleeping bag while it snowed. Those were some of my favorite sessions with some of the most profound answers.

Choices, choices. You can bring a camera and take photos to invite insight and a different kind of seeing OR after you go outdoors you can write down what you experienced OR both. What would feel most playful and delicious for you?

Other helpful hints: I highly suggest that this be a solo outing so you can bring your full presence to the time you are spending with nature. Make sure and be safe, okay? Take water, food, appropriate provisions and don't go anywhere that doesn't feel safe to go by yourself.

Before Your Medicine Walk

Define your question and/or intention. Where are you seeking insight and answers? What is alive in you and wanting clarification? Write down your question. I cannot state this enough. Do yourself a favor and write it down, and then forget about it until after you return from your Medicine Walk.

When you reach your destination (for hiking, sitting/meditating, kayaking, etc.) and you are ready to go, take a deep breath and set the intention to receive exactly what you need to receive. I invite you to say Thank You in advance for the wisdom that will be reflected to you in your experience.

Stay present and in a place of inner ease. Take photos or just notice what you notice around you and within you. Drop any agenda, including the question you are asking; just stay present and be with your experience. You don't need to look for answers, just be aware of what captures your attention both within you and around you. Trust that you will remember exactly what wisdom wants to come home with you. Simply enjoy your experience.

There are no wrong choices, just different outcomes.

After Your Medicine Walk

Take some notes, beautiful. Write in the first person and the present tense. For example: *I am* or *I imagine* or *I see* instead of *I was* or *I imagined* or *I saw.*

- **Describe what you saw,** recalling the details of your experience that stand out. No need to interpret anything at this point, just the facts, Ma'am.

- **What did you notice** about yourself and your experience? Your body, your emotions, your thoughts?

- **Look back over your noticings** with your question or intention in mind. What bone-deep wisdom is embedded in your descriptions?

- **What insights do you now have** about moving forward with your question/intention?

Take a moment to express appreciation for what you saw, your experience and the insight you've gained. Even if more questions came up, that's great insight as well.

Forever

by Claudia Cummins[v]

May you be steadied and supported
by the earth beneath your feet.

May you be nourished and energized
by the fires of life within.

May you be healed and opened
by the rivers of life that pour through.

May you be held and illuminated
by the light that shines everywhere
and forever.

nonajordan.com

surf lessons

Lesson Eight:
Full Presence Required

*I*n and on the water, there is nowhere but here. Well, really, that's true everywhere, but the ocean effortlessly invites that state of presence. The ocean is filled with exquisite silence, the endless roar of waves, and ever-shifting tides and currents; without full attention and presence, a wave may take you somewhere you don't want to go. When you are fully present, you become a co-creator working with the waves instead of against them.

I've learned that when I drop into my body and leave the descriptions, judgments and thinking behind, my attention leads me exactly where I need to go. When I'm on the water, or in the woods, mechanisms I don't understand and connections my DNA remembers come to life. I drop fully into the experience and live in the moment through my senses and instincts. When I experience my surroundings viscerally, through my senses instead of my thinking mind, I feel most alive, most deeply connected. I can trust that.

So can you.

When you bring your full presence to this moment, you connect to the nature all around you through your own nature. The whole ecosystem becomes both a mirror and a reflection of the truth you know in the deepest recesses of your soul but may not have access to in your mind – yet.

I'm not saying it's easy, but it is simple. In Full Presence, you will find exactly what you need, and it will be far richer than what you might find otherwise.

You Are Invited:
Practice Full Presence

The universe is full of magical things patiently waiting for our wits to grow sharper.

~Eden Phillpotts[vi]

Your invitation from the previous lesson stands – this lesson is all about your Medicine Walk and continuing your daily Core Practices.

With ease and grace, allow yourself to drop out of the mind when on your Medicine Walk and when playing. Allow yourself to simply be present to all that is within you and around you – let your entire body breathe in life. Connect to your own experience of yourself and the world via your senses and your soul-knowing – this is a portal to accessing your natural abundance, moment to moment.

It's worthwhile to note where it's easiest for you to drop out of your thinking mind and into your experience. For me, that state most easily comes when I am outdoors, especially surfing. How about you?

nonajordan.com surf lessons

Lesson Nine:
Never the Same

*A*s much as I may want to hold on to a certain experience or set of circumstances, nothing is ever the same way twice.

Every time I go to Electric Beach to snorkel, I notice I'm always surprised when the sand has shifted dramatically or the surf is different than I expect. I also seem to think the sea turtles will be in the same place every time. This happens every time to one degree or another – this expectation that the ocean will remain static. I am reminded over and over again by the playful, ever-changing ocean that everything about me, the people around me, my experience, the ocean and the earth – even the Universe – is in constant flux and flow.

When I remember that fundamental truth, it wakes me up. I open up to receive what the moment has to offer; the current experience is where the magic of synchronicity happens. These contrasting states – expecting things to remain static versus knowing change is the only constant – reminds me of the difference between using a tiny penlight to look for something versus a large flood lamp.

When I operate under the valid assumption that things are never exactly the same way twice, I drop into a state of openness and wonder that deeply connects me to natural abundance in each moment.

i thank You God for most this amazing

by e e cummings[vii]

i thank You God for most this amazing
day: for the leaping greenly spirits of trees
and a blue true dream of sky; and for
everything
which is natural which is infinite which is
yes

You Are Invited:
Develop Wonder

Have you completed your Medicine Walk? Are you continuing with your daily Core Practices? Are you finding that you embody playful energy and, therefore, natural abundance throughout your days?

Considering that what shows up on your Medicine Walk and during your daily play practice will never be repeated, can you drop into a state of full presence and a sense of wonder? Not only during your Core Practice but throughout your day as a way to access a natural state of abundance?

Can you absorb the present moment through your skin? Feast on it with your eyes? Drink it in?

What do you notice about your experience when you bring your full presence right here and open your eyes to this moment in wonder?

Lesson Ten:
Trust Your Rhythm

There are days I want to surf, but the ocean has something different in mind. Some days the water is smooth as glass with barely any waves, some days the surf is high and pounding and, frankly, dangerous for my beginner's skills. At first, I would be peeved and annoyed when the conditions weren't favorable to surfing. I wanted it to be just how I wanted it, all the time.

The ocean reminds me that nature is all about rhythms: seasons, tides, shadows and light. From the riotous colors of summer to the quiet whispers of death and decay in the depth of winter and everything in between, it is all part and parcel of nature – the nature around us reflects the natural rhythms within us.

We live in a world disconnected from the natural rhythms of life. Our culture expects constant growth, perpetual light, endless energy and non-stop performance. And so we have largely turned our backs on the wisdom and value of our own rhythms, our own seasons. Cut off from our natural rhythms, we assume that certain states or conditions are bad and should be avoided. We don't trust ourselves (or the process) when our bodies age or become ill, when we experience darkness or difficulty, when we encounter fallow times without inspiration, or when we find ourselves (consciously or unconsciously) dismantling our lives.

Living from natural abundance calls you home to the rich beauty and necessity of the full range and rhythm of your experience – calling attention to your infinite capacity to be at home with yourself in the world.

When you edge toward embracing the full range of experience as your playground without exception, you become unstoppable. You ARE nature. Bear witness to, and make room for, both the stormy seas and the calm waters within you.

Know that you are ALIVE.

Interlude

Part of taking risks, being brave, continually choosing ourselves, and diving headlong into play and pleasure is feeling it all the way through (which can be so, SO uncomfortable).

It takes courage to feel it all the way through, to let it move, to express it.

I can only speak to my experience, but I have never been a crier. I would say stoic is a good word for me when it comes to grief, pain, fear, sadness, etc.

About five years ago, I started to explore having feelings – like REALLY experiencing my feelings instead of eating them or shoving them aside. There was a LOT of catching up to do. I cried every day. I watched sad movies, I raged and shadowboxed while imagining myself kicking childhood adversaries' asses. It was hard for a few days and then, at some point, I realized when I let myself feel the full range of my feelings – whether sadness or joy or anger or grief – when I stopped telling myself a story about "good" feelings and "bad" feelings, then feeling felt like a vital piece of being alive.

Today, when my daughter and I are in the midst of a peak moment of joy or are experiencing the heartbreak of my husband being absent for his work, I often say to her, "This moment. These tears of joy or sorrow, this experience right here? This is how we know we are alive."

I know my capacity for happiness has grown AND my bravery has grown as I've become able to embrace and feel my emotions. I have less fear of my emotions and, in fact, see them as essential – I feel alive when I feel emotion course through my body.

You Are Invited:
Trust Your Rhythms

Today you are invited to trust your rhythms – to honor and claim the full range of your experience as valid and to act accordingly.

What would shift if you trusted yourself and your rhythms? What would you do differently if you trusted the whispers (or perhaps screams) of truth reflected to you in your unique rhythms: in your body, in your experience, in the nature within you and all around you?

Who would you be if you embraced it all, the full beat of your natural rhythms?

Lesson Eleven:
This is Home

Spending long periods of time in the waves reminds me at a cellular level that the ocean – a place of perpetual movement, creative response and play – is home.

One day I was at a favorite boogie-boarding beach with my daughter, Clara, and my husband, Erick. Though we went to boogie board "because Clara loves it," Clara spent the vast majority of the day digging in the sand while Erick and I stayed out on the waves nearly all day.

Knocked down, flipped over and crashed on happened. Effortless ease, perfect waves and long rides into shore happened. Seemingly endless streams of snot and seawater from my nose, laughter and *Oh shit, that wave is big* – yep, that all happened. Floating near my husband, waiting in silence, just feeling the water undulate beneath my body happened too.

I can say without a shadow of a doubt that every single moment on those waves was delicious and welcomed as I constantly played with, rode, dove into and responded to the water. This. Is. Home.

I love that when I spend time in and on the water, I can still feel the ocean moving inside me when I'm back on shore. It's as if the ocean within my body synchronizes with the oceans of earth and maintains its rocking sensation long after I've stepped out of the waves. I treasure that sweet reminder we are made of the same stuff, fractals of the earth herself.

We ARE nature. We are built for play. It is the heartbeat of creation, this ever-present, exquisite and delicious feast that is life. In my experience, the more I stay connected to this truth – to my true home – the less I fear and the more I trust. My actions are more purposeful. My intentions are clearer, though sometimes getting to them is messier. My process is wilder, more meandering and far more organic – but the results? Far more magnificent.

Connecting with your true nature and the nature all around forges an unshakable trust in yourself and it enhances your sense of natural abundance.

My deepest desire is that you are finding your way to that sacred place for yourself.

You Are Invited:
Come Home

On the heels of your Medicine Walk, as you are being playful and weaving it into your life—

Today you are invited to reflect on your experience of your own nature and the nature within and all around you.

Speak Your Truth

What do you know now about yourself (and perhaps your source of abundance) that you didn't know before?

Lesson Twelve:
The Wave Will Tell You
How to Ride It

When I first started boogie-boarding and surfing, I asked a lot of questions of the "experts" I saw rockin' the waves.

When do you catch a wave?

How do you know when to stand up?

What's the strategy to ride longer?

I had so many questions. And I wanted answers – a manual would have been preferable. But, without fail, the person I asked would say with a smile, "The wave will tell you how to ride it." It was so annoying.

But here's the deal: No one can tell you how to ride that wave; you just have to get out there and play. Experience it for yourself. Feel your way through it and learn how to listen to the thrum of the ocean. The mastery happens in my body, certainly not in my mind, and it is the truest thing I've ever experienced.

At the end of the day, despite the desire we ALL seem to have to look elsewhere for validation, information or expertise, there is no substitute for having your own experience.

And the wave? It will absolutely tell you how to ride it.

You Are Invited:
Listen to the Wave

Today you are invited to listen. To know your experience – not anyone else's experience – of play and pleasure, risk and visioning and of course, the unique heartbeat of your natural abundance.

Speak Your Truth

What are you carrying forward beyond *Surf Lessons*?

What has the wave of your life taught you about riding it?

Interlude

"I feel a part of nature. I feel nature is not only a source of metaphor, nature shows me the reality of life. (Do you feel the difference?)

Waves show me how energy moves. Trees show me roots, foundations, how to reach up and out, how to pluck what is needed from all around me and how to grow.

There are lunar cycles and seasons and years – in spirals, not straight lines – in-breaths and out-breaths, rest and growth.

I feel the tugs in my belly and I am more likely to follow them now; I am rewarded in small ways and big. I notice when I'm working too hard, I notice when I haven't played. I know the difference between rest and play and the value of each. I know I don't have to earn either, both are my birthright.

Learning to sing makes me happy in a way so out of proportion to what you'd expect. Even though it's hard and my voice is not conditioned (i.e., sounds bad), I keep crying with happiness at my lessons and when I even think about my lessons. And don't get me started about surfing. Singing + surfing = I'm a BADASS.

I stand up straighter and look people in the eye more often. I feel bigger, freer to be me, to take up space and to be heard. I have been on a very slow path of growth, Nona Jordan, but YOU have catalyzed big changes in my life. (That is your genius). I am so grateful."

-Allison Evans

Lesson Thirteen:
It Is All for You

My family moves a lot for my husband's work, and I struggle with resentment around that periodically. There have been places we've lived where I haven't really "lived" there at all.

In those times and spaces, I was tightly contracted without an ounce of gratitude or contentment. I was locked away in bitterness, waiting for things to go my way, for circumstances to be what I wanted them to be.

I didn't "want" Hawai'i either. The schools aren't great, it's expensive, locals aren't very friendly, etc. The list of reasons not to connect? Well, I can always write a list that feels watertight.

It was hard when we got here, and then I chose to step out. I couldn't stand to tell myself the same old tired stories. I desperately wanted a different way to be with the constant flux of our life – I chose to surf.

At the end of my first lesson, I sat on the beach and looked out at the surf. It was as if every move my family ever made was rushing toward me on the waves – the good ones, the great ones, the shitty ones – and then all of my judgments, all of my ideas about the places we've been, fell away.

All of a sudden the thought washed up, "This is all for me." This. This is for me. This life, this experience – with its adventure and its exhaustion, the deserts and the oceans, the storms and the sunshine, its exasperation and its acceptance, its tears and its howls of laughter... it is all for me.

Every single bit of it is for me. My surf lesson.

A moment of grace opened up for me then. I finally understood that it was my choice, that nature, that life, is always inviting me to dance. Sometimes I get to pick the music, and sometimes nature asks me to show up and play with what is. Either way, I get to choose.

Now I can't get enough. Now I want to embrace life in a way that leaves the world a richer place, that leaves ripples in the hearts and lives of those around me.

Not only is it all for me, but it's all for you, too – the endless, infinite wellspring of natural abundance.

Go to the Limits of Your Longing

by Rainer Maria Rilke[viii]

God speaks to each of us as he makes us,
then walks with us silently out of the night.

These are the words we dimly hear:

You, sent out beyond your recall,
go to the limits of your longing.
Embody me.

Flare up like flame
and make big shadows I can move in.

Let everything happen to you: beauty and
terror.
Just keep going. No feeling is final.
Don't let yourself lose me.

Nearby is the country they call life.
You will know it by its seriousness.

Give me your hand.

You Are Invited:
It Is All for You

Today you are invited to embody and express your gratitude for the infinite wellspring of natural abundance. To appreciate the ways in which life, nature, the world, even the Universe, are all for you…

Thank You for Surfing with Me

*I*f this book has inspired you to open your heart a bit wider to living the life you most want to live, I would love a review at your online retailer, or please send me feedback or a note at nona@nonajordan.com - I look forward to hearing from you.

Sharing your experience may inspire people to read this book and find that a life of playful, natural abundance is something they can have, too.

I wholeheartedly believe we can start a revolution of delight. The more people who unapologetically embrace play and pleasure as their birthright, the saner, healthier and happier we humans, and our planet, will be now and in the future.

I want that for all of us.

Surf on.

xoxo . nona

Acknowledgments

There is an African proverb you've likely heard that says, "It takes a village to raise a child." I would contend that it takes a village and an entire ecosystem of love and attention for just about anything worthwhile to come to fruition, even a book of meditations on life as modest as this.

I want to honor the many human teachers and guides who encouraged me to rediscover the instinctual joy and abundance of my true nature.

Thank you to Michael and Lynn Trotta of Sagefire Institute, who gently nudged me back outdoors through a regular Sit Spot practice and nature-based coach training. I will be forever grateful to both of you for inspiring me and waking something inside of me I didn't even realize was asleep. So much of this process grew out of the practices that I cultivated for myself while studying with you, Michael. You can learn more about Michael at SageFireInstitute.com.

As I was rediscovering myself and nature in new ways, I was led to you, Pixie Lighthorse. Your wisdom teachings have been a rich source of connection with nature and the creative pulse of divine feminine in myself and in the world. I am grateful to you and honored to be among your first Earth Medicine Shamanic Practitioners.

Ronna Detrick encouraged me to capture the lessons of the sea. Without you, Ronna, *Surf Lessons* would never have come to pass as a course or as this volume. I am ever grateful for the abundance of women in my life who affirm my voice. May I do the same for other women as often as possible.

My endless thanks to Erick, who encouraged me to take my first surf lesson and enthusiastically supported my desire to surf. Erick, from the bottom of my heart, thank you for always and forever supporting me in my desire to know life more deeply through rich experiences. Thank you for always standing by my side and saying Yes.

My heart swells like the waves of the ocean when I think about my daughter, Clara, who inspires me to keep going, to keep deepening my understanding of what it means to be a powerful woman. With any luck, she will live in a world with fewer constraints than I grew up believing were truth. Plus, Clara, you are always up for a good adventure, and I love that about you. Thank you for choosing me to be your mom – what an honor and privilege.

I would be remiss if I didn't mention Allison Evans and family – fondly known as "The Allisons". Thank you, thank you, thank you. I couldn't have asked for better friends to play with in Hawai'i.

Finally, my thanks for my team of badass technical warriors. Without them, none of this would be possible. My deepest gratitude to both Crys Wood, Jen Falci and the Michelle Vandepas team at Grace Point Publishing. My work would never go anywhere without you.

Perhaps it goes without saying, but the greatest honor and thanks I have is for the earth herself – the original Mother. I feel such deep gratitude and awe for the beauty and wealth you freely share. The wisdom teachings nature invites me to know through my experience inspire me to keep exploring. The resilience and creative genius of nature are truly a marvel to behold. I could not be more honored and delighted to be here, right now, with all of you, spinning through space, held by the Mother.

Thank you. Thank you. Thank you.

ENDNOTES:

---

[i] Deeper Than Words: Living the Apostles' Creed Paperback – June 15, 2010

[ii] INSECURE AT LAST: Losing It in Our Security-Obsessed World by Eve Ensler. Copyright © 2006 by Random House Inc.

[iii] Circle of Grace: A Book of Blessings for the Seasons by Jan Richardson, ©2015 Wanton Gospeller Press, Permission granted by the author.

[iv] The Gift: Poems by Hafiz, The Great Sufi Master by Hafiz, translated by Daniel Ladinsky ©1999 Penguin Books Inc.

[v] Forever by Claudia Cummings, Permission granted by the author

[vi] A Shadow Passes by Eden Phillpotts, ©1929 Cecil Palmer & Hayward, London. (HathiTrust)

[vii] I thank You God for this most amazing by e e cummings, Originally published
in Xaipe1 (New York: Oxford University Press, 1950), reissued in 2004 by Liveright, an imprint of W.W. Norton & Company.

[viii] Rilke's Book of Hours: Love Poems to God, translated by Anita Barrows and Joanna Macy, ©1997, Riverhead Books